Being Heard: Healing Voices of Trauma

A Collection of Writings

Vera Stasny

BALBOA.
PRESS

A DIVISION OF HAY HOUSE

Balboa Press books may be ordered through booksellers or by contacting:

Balboa Press
A Division of Hay House
1663 Liberty Drive
Bloomington, IN 47403
www.balboapress.com
1 (877) 407-4847

Print information available on the last page.

ISBN: 978-1-9822-0790-8 (sc)
ISBN: 978-1-9822-0789-2 (e)

Balboa Press rev. date: 12/07/2018

CONTENTS

DEDICATION

This collection of poems is dedicated to the many souls who, like me, have experienced and confronted trauma in their own lives, who are wanting to go deeper within, to be vulnerable, and willing to explore their world through a new lens.

For my mother,

Elizabeth

In loving memory

TRAUMA

Snippets of memory.
Emotions vivid and too frightening
haunt and disrupt us.

Will we dare to reveal them?
Or keep them buried in the recesses of our brains and
trapped in our bodies?

Hidden away in a murky space.
Fuzzy details surround us.
The emotional insult becomes vivid as the drama is recalled.

Breathing becomes difficult.
A gaping mouth,
frightened eyes,
may reveal the horror of the experience
as we try to process the old event.

We can confront these memories
and heed the call to attention
to let them go,
and discharge what keeps us stuck, frozen, damaged.

trauma | ˈtroumə, ˈtrômə |

noun (plural **traumas** or **traumata** | -mətə |)

1 a deeply distressing or disturbing experience: *a personal trauma like the death of a child.*
   * emotional shock following a stressful event or a physical injury, which may be associated with physical shock and sometimes leads to long-term neurosis.

2 *Medicine* physical injury.

ORIGIN
....
late 17th century: from Greek, literally 'wound'.

WITH GRATITUDE AND ACKNOWLEDGEMENT

To the many souls who I have encountered on my way,
Who have been part of my journey,
Who enlightened me,
Who taught and comforted me.
They played, laughed, and cried with me.

With Special Thanks to:

Susi, my soulmate, my twin, my most loyal, diligent and ardent supporter, who "has had my back" at all times, and helped make this collection possible; my everlasting gratefulness.

Harriett, my earth guide, who encouraged me to feel.
Laine, who urged me to keep a journal.
Caroline, who helped me see life through a different lens.
Michele, who gave me great insights for my debut writings.
Lisa T, who challenged me to be seen.
Noushin, at whose holiday party I shared my resolution to publish, that allowed this book to become a reality.
Marilyn, who reviewed my poetry, helped me refine it, and is an amazing teacher.

The many caring doctors and nurses who gave me yet another chance at life.

My family and friends for their inspiration, acceptance, patience, and love. Some of the poems were written for them.

And mostly, The Divine, which opened a portal allowing me occasional glimpses of my soul.

INTRODUCTION

This collection was born out of my personal story of trauma—from childhood to my senior years—which includes complex, chronic and intergenerational traumas as well. I was acutely aware of some of these past events, but did nothing to deal with them—other than getting through each one. Amazingly, I did not think my behavior was unusual, nor labeled my experiences as traumatic. I just numbed out, hovering "near" my body, without really inhabiting it.

My first inkling that I might be suffering from trauma happened while volunteering with my sister several years ago for an organization that supported military personnel returning home with PTSD. In a flash of recognition, it dawned on me that in a very small way, I had exhibited some of the same characteristics as those Vets.

Looking back I realized that my earliest introduction into this world was traumatic. My parents, who fled to England as Hitler marched into their Czechoslovakian homeland, were able to escape from the Nazis days before the outbreak of WWII, saving their own lives. They never saw their families again and were never certain what had actually happened to them until years later.

Their traumas became mine. As an infant in war-torn London, I was often rushed into shelters where the sounds of air-raid sirens, accompanied by shelling and bombings, haunted our beings. Food was rationed; uncertainty and fear was everywhere. Leaving England after the war, we emigrated to America, joining the few remaining survivors of a once large family.

Growing up, I had many health challenges that continued into adulthood—ovarian cancer and a total hysterectomy at age 21, a shattered pelvis from a ski accident, multiple other injuries, surgeries and the usual illnesses, as well as on-going autoimmune diseases.

When I became a caregiver for my mother, I witnessed her declining memory with both horror and compassion as she struggled with dementia. During this time she went from home-care to daycare, to assisted living and ultimately long-term care. I kept asking myself why she lingered for so long. I found my answer: In caring for her, I learned to open my heart. She became my teacher. It was her sacrifice, her unspoken, precious gift to me. In her own way she taught me to love, to give, to cherish, to accept, and to not judge.

After my mother died, I thought that I was "home free". I was exhausted from the combination of a high-stress job and from fifteen years of caregiving. I had enough.

Barely six weeks after her death, my cardiologist sent me to see a heart surgeon—my mitral valve was badly leaking. The coincidence came as complete surprise. The fact that heart surgery was required so soon after my mother's death was a wakeup call.

The news sent me into a tailspin. I was terrified. I panicked. I couldn't contain myself. My nights were disturbed. I slept fitfully, if I slept at all. During the day I was numb and barely functioning, looking like a zombie. I wasn't expecting yet more trauma. I thought that I had done my healing work, that I was a conscious, evolved human being on a path. I was blindsided.

I was waiting for surgery and my fear was mounting. That's when my friend Laine encouraged me to start journaling; so began my writing that continues to this day. This became my way of coping with all the emotions that were cascading, catapulting, and interrupting my days and nights. Writing became my way of expressing myself, of freeing myself, of calming myself.

I can't sit down to purposely write. It comes of its own volition. Sometimes I write in the middle of the night, or in the waiting room of a doctor's office, or while riding on the subway. Sometimes I stop whatever I am doing to write. Then, when I read my words later on, I don't quite know who wrote them. But they are my words. They are the channeled words that come through me.

The writings are about love, fear, loss, memories, joy, sadness, death, injustice, existence, and the soul. Some were promoted by events I witnessed, or by books that moved me and awakened intense emotions.

It felt important to me to share my story. I am not unique. Trauma is part of the collective human experience that none of us escape. My traumas, hidden within my body, affected my responses to the everyday challenges of my life's journey. Whether it was a big "T" or a little "t" trauma, it shaped, taught, inspired and empowered me.

When I was in college, I told a friend that I wanted to leave my mark on the world somehow. I didn't know quite what that would look like or if it was even remotely possible. Perhaps it was my unconscious and unrecognized desire "to be seen" that I had managed to tuck away almost forever.

It is now more than 50 years since I uttered those words. Finally I have found my voice. I hope my writings will resonate with you and reveal universal emotions. This will be my legacy in my infinitesimally small world.

June 2018

Allow my poetry to speak to you.
Find what feelings resonate.

Let it disturb you.
Let it challenge you.
Let it provoke you.
Let it inspire you.
Let it bring up your own memories as well...

PROLOGUE

I sit here wanting to write,
trying to find the portal.
Hoping a portal will open
so that some words of wisdom
will emanate from my being.

But nothing comes.
I can not force it.
I can not will it.

Hooded, Closed.
I need Patience.
I need Hope that inspiration will flow.

I need to be quiet and still
so that my heart will open again
for those brief moments...

It is not my writing after all.
It is the writing from the Divine.

AFTERMATH

How brilliant the mind is--
It finds a way to cope.
It wants to come home.

It lashes out.
It screams.
Jittery, jumpy.

It numbs itself out.
One dimensional.
Flat.
Gone.

Terror and rage is
lurking behind an invisible wall.

Look for safe ground.
Find an entrance
to the interior.
Find a way in.
Find a path.

Trust.
You can heal your demons.
You have the desire to heal.
You have the will to survive.
You already have the courage.

(Wounded Warriors. PTSD)

AMERICAN DREAM

Have we grown too big?
Have we grown too strong?
Can't we see our own creations?

Cracks are beginning to show.

The strain is taking its toll on all.

Madness
Rage
Frustration
Fear
Revenge
Apathy

Can't we solve this?

America is unwinding.

ANACHRONISM

In a flash we respond to a new stimulus
with an out-dated, old familiar response.

It is a hair-trigger reaction
that renders the innocent bystander speechless.

This reaction is out of context.
From another time.

This wound stays buried
in the graveyard of memories.
Until it is scratched open again.

It is an old wound
carelessly or purposefully shoved onto the listener
in the present moment.

ANGELS ON THE LOOSE

You never know when they will appear.
You never know what they will look like.

They are all around you waiting to be recognized.
They are all around you wanting to help.
They are all around you wanting to bestow their light,
their love, their gift.

They are your friends and family who are always there
for you.
They flutter their wings—over and over again.

They are the doctors and the nurses who care for you.
They too flutter their wings.

They could be anyone, anywhere...
They are the strangers or acquaintances who flutter their
wings even for a brief moment.

They smile.
They reassure.
They touch your arm.
They offer words of comfort.
They remind you that you are not alone.
They don't know that they have touched you.

And they don't know that they too are angels.

(My hospital stay)

BLIND SPOT

A void emerges.
It is that place at the end of a psychic trail
where you can't go.
You don't dare.

It is a unspoken boundary imposed upon you
which is an unwritten stop sign in the conversation.

It is a barrier
which holds you hostage to those unwritten rules.

The flow stops.
The music stops.
It constricts.
It distorts.
It cancels.

So you sigh,
Suck in your breath.
And hold your tongue
to avoid an argument
to save the relationship.

BLITZKRIEG

There is noise everywhere.
Crashing, rumbling, discordant.
Screeching sirens, falling bombs.

It is not safe here.
I have entered into
a dangerous world.

Cradled in the arms of a traumatized being
who attempts to shield me from what is,
to offer me protection, comfort and love.

My toes curl upward.
They don't want to touch this unsafe ground.

I don't want to feel
this existential terror that envelops me.
I recoil at the slightest disturbance.

Hush little baby, don't you cry...

BROKEN HEART

BODYMINDSPIRIT

Trinity.
One word.
No separation.

A spirit crying
A soul crying
A universe crying
No separation.

A body crying
A heart crying
A mind crying
No separation.
Heart strings broken.

"PAY ATTENTION !" the soul cries.
"I WILL !" replies the body.
And IT does.
No separation.
Heart strings broken.

"PAY ATTENTION!" the body cries.
And IT does.
No separation.
Heart strings broken.

"I will"
"I WILL!" cries the mind.
The mind gets it at last.
No separation.
Heart strings broken.

(On heart surgery)

CHAOS

In a futile attempt we try to control the outer world
in order to manage the chaos that exists in our mind.

When the inner landscape is in turmoil,
then the outer world must be its opposite
in order to protect.

But we limit this view of the outer world
by the chaos within.

Trying to control the outer world
to fix a broken inside won't work.
Because we can never create perfection...

No amount of vigilance can mend the inner landscape.
It is an illusion.

But there is hope.
If we draw attention inward.
And we are willing.
And there is an opening.

Chaos is just another unseen wound.

CHILDLESS

A numb heart.
An empty womb.

A stolen future.
A different path.

Children have left the nest.
I am now like everyone else.

But I am wrong.
First there are children, then grandchildren,
then great-grandchildren.

Not for me.
Never to be.

Who will grieve for me?
No headstone for me.
Weep no tears.

My arms are still empty.
My heart is a broken heart.

CRISIS

A game changer.
  It demands from you that you act
    in a totally different way,
      in an unfamiliar way,
        in a new way.

It demands that you take action.

It demands that you move forward.

It demands your presence.

without a guide book,
without rules,
without a plan.
without knowing the outcome.

It is a like a lightening bolt that emerges out of a
darkness.
This crisis illuminates a new landscape.

THE DANCE

What happened to us?
You stopped me in my tracks when we met.
I saw no one else.

You were my perfection.
I was yours.

I didn't really see you then.
I didn't see me.
I didn't see our differences.

The delight I once felt has changed
to a quiet contentment.

Can we dance again once more?

(On old relationships)

DEFENSES

Survive
Protect
Contract
Pull in.

Here it comes again—
Unexpected attacks
Unconscious behaviors.

The Criticizer attacks:
You are doing it wrong.
Contract.

The Protector smothers:
You have no room, no space.
Crawl away.

The Achiever takes the spotlight:
Does it all.
Fade into the shadows.

The Romantic is wrapped up in drama and
self-expression:
There is no place for you on this stage.
Disappear.

The Observer, your mirror:
Two souls meet with so much space between.
Neither willing to be seen.
Both hearts shrivel.

The Worrier, so busy living in the imagined future:
Never sees the present, never sees the presenter.
Reassure.

The Enthusiast, a Peter Pan:
Won't make choices, lives like a hummingbird, trusting
nothing.
Dismay.

The Bossy one: anger ..."don't mess with me".
Help! Run for cover.
Don't get hit with that rage.
Contract.

The Procrastinator:
Blur, miasma. Can't really see you, so you don't matter.
Frustration.

Wounds.
Wounds.

Pain all around.
Is it real?

Go within.
Look to the light.
Go to the Divine..

*(One soul's response to different wounds and coping
patterns of others...based on the Enneagram)*

DESPERATION

Decision:

The human will to survive
drives victims of war, bigotry, and intolerance
to escape the reality of murder, massacre, torture, rape,
slavery
which lurks ever-present in the shadows.

Misery:

So they leave their beloved homeland
by any means
begging for help.
Hoping someone will help.

Treachery:

They are often betrayed.
Frightened, they press on.
The unknown future better than the known past.

Barriers:

Mountains.
Oceans.
Deserts.
Unscrupulous rescuers
slow the way.
A constant danger.
even deadly.

Refusal:

Arriving at what seems like a safe haven,
they are turned away,
turned back,
held in camps or prisons,
refused.

Devastation:

Tribal warfare.
Indifference.
God against God.
Will it ever end?

Epic:

A story unfolding today
that has been repeated over and over again

century after century,
tribe against tribe,
people against people,
country after country.

Our humanity is at stake.

(refugee crises from wars and genocide)

DID I TOUCH YOU?

When I no longer walk upon this earth
and I leave you behind...

Will you remember me?
Will you hold me in your heart?
Will you smile in those moments
when you are reminded of me?
Will you cherish me?

Will you say I made you laugh?
Will you say I made you cry?
Will you say I made you angry?

Will you say I helped you understand?
Will you say I taught you something?

Will you say I loved you?
Will you hold me in your heart?

Then...I have touched you.

DO YOU KNOW ME?

When you were small you saw me through the eyes of a child.

But do you know me?

Then you were grown and on your own.
You had glimpses of me.
But you were busy with your own children.

But do you know me?

Now I am aging.
My hair is turning gray.
Soon I will need your care and help.

But do you know me?

Please don't wait
until it is too late.
When I no longer know me.

END OF THE ROAD

We have said all we can say to each other.
We have exhausted our repertoire, our conversation.

Our dialogue has become repetitive.
Even mundane.
Events are unimportant.
Details become the focus.
Feelings become suppressed.

We have lost our connection.
Yet we still have our memories
of times we have shared,
of moments we have treasured.

It is over.
We can't do this any longer.
We have hit a brick wall.

(On old relationships)

ENDANGERED SPECIES

Will we protect our endangered species?

Not only the birds in the sky
Or the animals in the jungle
Or the fish in the ocean
Or the plants and flowers that grow in the earth.

But our young Black and Brown men
Our Immigrants
The Impoverished
The Forgotten
Who might be subject to police brutality
Simply because of who they are.

Or will we continue to look the other way?
Unconscious of their plight.
Unconcerned about their dilemmas.
Indifferent to their harsh reality.

Comfortable in our own ways.
Safe with our privilege.
Smug in the status quo.
Filtering out what doesn't serve our beliefs.

(on bigotry and hate)

FEAR

I alternate between being distracted,
Somewhere,
Anywhere.

And then I am back
to feel the terror:

My breath short.
My chest tight.
My heart beating.

Then I fly out of my body:
Somewhere.
Anywhere.

Time goes by.
I don't know how much time:

Seconds.
Minutes.
Hours.

And then the terror strikes again:

My breath short.
My chest tight.
My heart beating.

The hurtling back and forth—
An endless battle.

Nameless.
Wordless.
Visceral.
Existential.

THE FOREST OF *MY SOUL*

I am lost in the middle of an unseen forest
that shrouds my vision,
blocks my way,
and veils my reality.

Why can't I see all that there is?
How can I find my way?
I have placed shrouds around me
and put myself in this forest of darkness.

I want to cast off these shrouds
so that I might know my soul,
dwell in my soul,
feel my soul.
And welcome it back home to me.

After all, my soul has been with me all the time.
It has never left me.
It still whispers to me.

Ah! To walk ahead together in this life.

FORGIVENESS

I forgive you.
I forgive you.
I forgive you.

I forgive me.

Please forgive me.
Please forgive me.
Please forgive me.

(For my father)

THE GAME

The cat attacks...it strikes out with its paw...
It hits the sleeping dog's leg.
The dog retreats.
It does not want to get caught.

The cat attacks again...
The dog retreats.
It gets up and moves away.
Farther.
Away.

The cat attacks again...
still not understanding why
he cannot engage the dog in his game.

The dog lunges at the cat...

The cat retreats, licks its wounds...
till next time...

Then the cat becomes the dog...
And the dog becomes the cat...

And so it goes.

(For my sister)

ICH BIN JUDE

These words bring tears to my eyes.

The testimony of survivors...

It is my secret.

It is my loss.

It is my sadness, my trauma,

My identity, my DNA.

My memory.

My legacy.

It changes my destiny.

It changes my language, my country.

It changes my family.
It changes me...

I must own it.
I must claim it.
I must reclaim it.

Never forget....

ICH BIN JUDE.

—

(On the Holocaust)

IF I DIE BEFORE YOU

It is because I could not bear to live without you.

If I die before you ...
It is because life's journey would not be the same
without you.

If I die before you ...
It is because my heart would break without you.

If I die before you ...
It is because I didn't have the courage to stand alone
without you.

If I die before you ...
It is because I believed that you could stand alone,
without me.

If I die before you ...
I know I will disappoint you....

Can you ever forgive me
If I die before you.

(In Memoriam)

THE JUKEBOX

The orderly mind plays the record of life in sequential order.

The demented mind plays the records in random order, in no order, in unseen order.

These records are our memories, our emotions, our experiences and our language.

It is still ours, it is still to be treasured, longing to be remembered.

Let it play...
don't take it away.

(On Dementia)

LOST SOULS

I am walking in all the familiar places
where we walked together.

I am looking for you.
I can feel you around me.
I can sense your presence.
I can see your smile.
I can hear your voice.

So I keep coming coming back here.
Hoping somehow to find you again.
Even though I cannot.
Hoping to catch a glimpse of you...

To catch a glimpse of what we once shared.

Oh, why did you leave me?

(In Memoriam)

LOVING YOU

Allow me to love you
Allow me to see you
Allow me to feel you

Nothing to do
Nothing to change
Time after time

Strip away the fear
Strip away the facade
Strip away the defenses
Strip away the mask

I will love you forever
Just as you are
Time after time.

MEDDLING

Well meaning advice
Well meaning concern
Well meaning alarm

From well wishers
From friends and family

All trying to help you.
Correct you, change you, make you wrong...

It may have no positive outcome whatsoever.
With no practical solutions that you don't already know,
Which you haven't already considered.

But everyone once in a while a nugget reveals itself.

So you listen, nod your head.
Take it in with a patient smile.

The meddler is none the wiser for having meddled.
And you deal with whatever is on your plate the best way
you can.

And then one day you become the meddler:
Well-meaning.
Well-intentioned.
You offer well-meaning advice.
Well-meaning concern.

Well-meaning alarm to others.
Who in turn listen, nod their heads
With a patient smile.

Still falling on deaf ears.

MELODIES

I hear a faint song coming from somewhere.

It triggers a memory,

a memory of you.

A time, a place, a moment.

I recall an emotion

from a long time ago.

Yet it is as vivid and as real as yesterday.

A tear forms on my eyelid

And drops onto my cheek.

(In Memoriam)

METAMORPHOSIS

A soul in the wings

A soul readying

A soul yearning

A soul giving

A soul loving

A soul ascending

A soul resting.

A soul in the wings...

MISSING YOU

The past gets stripped away.

Only the present moment survives.

Remnants of the past tumble out occasionally.

Then the familiar becomes a source of comfort.

Solace.

A sweetness emerges through the dimming light of awareness.

A vulnerability.

An innocence.

We mourn for what lies ahead.

With the knowledge of the robbery yet to come.

For the heartbreak ahead...

When there is no turning back.

Mercy.

(On Dementia)

THE MOVIE

Our minds are constantly filled with our own thoughts.
And we believe them.
Completely.

Our struggles and fears are of our own Creation.
So creative that we don't realize that we are the
director
scriptwriter
editor
film maker
casting the perfect actors.
for our reruns.

We repeat the script—
with new actors
and new episodes.

It is our illusion, our story
that can be altered in a moment.

The End.

NOISE IN MY HEAD

The days come and go.
I laugh.
I enjoy.
I forget.

I awaken in the middle of the night with
Worry
Fear
Anxiety
To accompany me.
To disturb my sleep.

The possibilities,
The worst-case scenarios,
Buzz in my head
And disturb my sleep.

My unconscious is smarter than my conscious,
It forces me to deal with the here and now...

But my imagination runs wild.
It torments me until I let go.
It torments me until I fall asleep.

Those are the cruelest hours.
It is when I grieve
for what was,
for what is,
for what could have been,
for what might be.

PAIN

Help me help me help me

Help, me. Help. Me . HELP. ME.

Help help help me me me....

HELP ME

Agh.

THE PAPER BAG

I have placed a paper bag over my head,
I tie it tightly.
Then fill it with my own thoughts and creations—
Hieroglyphs
which I have constructed
from my own personal angst.

I am the painter,
the molder,
the shaper,
the architect.

Yet this illusion
holds me,
limits me,
stifles me,

I need more space.
I need relief.
I am suffocating.

PARTICIPATION

I feel powerless.
I am reminded of my vulnerability,
of my own fragility.
Of my mortality.

I look beyond myself.
Vulnerable.
It is the randomness.

Let them help you.
Let them be there for you.
Let them love you.

It is what they want to do.

POST SURGERY

My body is in shock.

It has been invaded by metals, chemicals, liquids.

Cameras capture everything on the inside, magnified.

The surgeons cut and paste, sew, trim, tighten.

Humpty Dumpty put back together.

Even if I don't know it intellectually,
my body fully comprehends.

It is a planned assault.

I am wounded.

It will be a seemingly endless healing process.

Some gains...lots of effort.

Only time will tell.

PUPPETRY

Unseen strings move us.
We think we are self-directed,
of our own free will.

Perhaps we recognize that a string is being pulled--
Even if the recognition is fleeting.
Perhaps we can slow our reactions,
or modify them.

Bound by the strings that tug us this way
then that.

But it is an illusion,
a learned survival skill.

We are puppets
of a script written and then rewritten.
A cosmic laugh!

It is a wake-up call!

REVELATION

I shared my story with you
trusting you to keep it safe
because I could not contain it.
Too much emotion--

Hiding my indiscretion.
Hiding my imperfection.
Hiding my weakness.

I shared my secret with you,
hoping you would not forget your promise.
Trusting you to keep it safe.

Then you shared my secret with a trusted friend,
you, trusting them to guard it well.
Who shared it yet again.
Too much.

Now my story has been told and retold.
Sharing my indiscretion.
Sharing my imperfection.
Sharing my weakness.

And in the end I did not die.

RECUPERATION

How did I get here?
The doctor discharges me
to return to normal life as before.

But I can't return to what was.
What IS becomes the theme of the day.

Reality has a new face.
Will my body support me?
Can I trust it?
Will I have to comprise something?

Will people really see ME
Or will they see only the patient?

Either not understanding what I went through
and expecting more...

Or assuming I am finished, old, washed up
and will need to be handled with kid gloves.

ROLLER COASTER

I am calm, relaxed...
then some thought enters unannounced into my
consciousness
and the panic sets in.

I stop breathing properly and start holding my breath.
My stomach churns.

My muscles tighten; my heart feels like it is burning up.
My throat constricts and I can barely talk.
The color drains out of my face.

I need to do something.
Distract myself...eat chocolate,
go shopping, watch TV.
Something to quiet my thoughts.
Anything.

Probably meditation and quiet music would be better.

Instead I seek more information
which keeps me on heightened alert.
I am like a chicken without a head.
Disconnected.

This is not in the realm of the intellect...on the contrary.
It is the catalyst that travels to the emotional body via the physical...
and wreaks its havoc.

Then I am so tired from this self-induced torment.
Did these toxic reactions—triggered by my thoughts—
flood my system?

I am drowning in a non-specific panic that is only visible from within.
I have managed to hide it away from onlookers.

That's when I need to reach out,
to talk to someone who is not in a panicked state
so I can mirror that calm presence.
Or take a nap and sleep it off.

Then the calm returns....until the next attack.

SECOND CHANCE

A heart can only contract for so many years before the muscles fatigue under the pressure...

The energy required to hold back, to hold in, to restrict, is like a dam that finally collapses under the strain...

A heart hidden away by an invisible wall is a broken heart.

It can be repaired.

It can be mended.

It can be restored.

This is an invitation.

The surgeon's hand can fix the physical...

But it requires a lifetime of work to be willing to stop the holding back.

It can happen in an instant.

It can reveal a tender, gentle heart.

Freedom.

Breath.

The gift of life.

The joy of life.

Maybe it was visible all along...

Now my heart can sing again.

SHOCK WAVE

Something happens to alter your reality.
   ...Everything shifts.

This new reality is totally different from a moment ago.

Whatever you thought was unchangeable,
unmanageable,
unmovable,
set in stone,
... is gone.

A moment ago becomes meaningless, ,
Irrelevant,
...unimportant.

Unravel the mundane,
deal with this new paradigm.

Move,
move on,
move forward.

SILENCE

Away from the high-speed race
Away from the city crowds
Away from the city noise
Away from the city smells

Into the greenery
Into the mountains
Into the vastness
Into the allowing

Return to knowing
Return to being
Return to peace
Return to myself

SLAVES

We are unconscious—
unwittingly duped into a form of slavery
by our system, by our media,
by our belief and constructs.

Held captive to institutions,
to fashion, to medicine,
to education, to government, to tradition.
We submit willingly yet unknowingly....
All part of a paradigm
which we conform to and obey.

Destined to be repeated over and over again.

SOUL

How do we really know it?
How do we touch it?
The voice of our soul.

Have we come so far from listening
that we no longer know it even exists?
The voice of our soul.

Yet it is that voice that can liberate us,
forgive us, understand us,
inspire us –

Which recognizes us in our darkest, most solitary
moments.
It whispers to us.
The voice of our soul...

STANDING IN THE RAIN

Here I am
Standing in the rain.
All alone.

Sometimes I notice the rain.
Sometimes I feel it trickling down my face.
Sometimes.

I don't know how I got here.
I don't what I am doing here.
Nor for how long I have been here.

I only know that I am numb —
As if I could somehow freeze time.

It is my best strategy for coping without you.

It is my only strategy.

It is a stark reminder that I am still here.

Standing in the rain without you.

(For Lisa, In Memoriam for Dave)

STARDUST

We are made of star dust.
Like everything else on our planet.
The same elements as all the galaxies in our Universe.
How can we think we are the only beings...?
How can we not get it?

We are made of stardust.
The same as the creatures that roamed the earth
thousands of years ago.
They were stardust too.
Now they are long gone from the planet...
How can we not get it?

We are made of stardust.
The same forces that created the Universe over billions
of years ago, are still at work.
We are part of the whole, seen or unseen...
How can we not get it?

Will we too disappear from this planet some day...?
How can we not get it?

STEAM ROLLER

I shared my thoughts with you today,

Expecting you to receive them as a precious gift.

Instead you discarded them and threw them away.

Not caring,
Not wondering,
Not interested.

Your own precious thoughts steam-rolled over mine and crushed me.

STOLEN BODIES

What happens when one group sees itself as better than
another?
As superior to?
In charge of?
Controller of?

Contempt.
Indifference.
Violation.
Injustice.
Murder.

Only our minds are free.
Our bodies are subject to the rules of the powerful,
and the laws of the land,
that hijack Justice and Innocence.

Victims of genocide,
Enslaved people,
Prisoners,
Witnesses to war,
Activists,
Each know this truth.

They are wanting to be safe,
yearning to be set free.
Waiting for a hopeful tidal change.

SUPPORT

I am being held
in the arms of my friends and family.
Quietly embraced by the Divine.
Just let go and let them hold me.

Though it is my journey,
I don't have to walk it totally alone.
It doesn't have to be so solitary.

TIME STANDS STILL

Routine.
Daily grind.
Going through the motions.

Boredom.

On the job.
Day-in, day-out.
Year after year.

Complacency.

Cut corners.
Compromise.
Minor infractions.
Look the other way.

Carelessness.

Until something out of the ordinary happens.
Then you get caught in the headlights.

Judged.

Your actions are now under a microscope.
Now charged with a crime.
Convicted of being human.

Guilty.

(The escape from Dannemora Prison: The Prison Guard)

TOXIC DUMP

Held hostage by another's mood.
We can not escape the negativity
which infiltrates the air
with a sickening stillness.

And the offender, withdrawn
Is unaware.
The effect is as potent just the same.

It leaves us agitated.
Disturbed.
Uncomfortable.

Wanting to reach out.
Not knowing what to do.
Not knowing how to help.
Not knowing if to help.

It's a gotcha.

THE VEIL

Everything looks so normal.
Everyone getting along—or not.
But yet somehow it is not authentic.

There is a forgotten skill,
A lost intimacy.
An inability to communicate.
So we stop at a safe distance.

But if we listen carefully, observe, and can penetrate the
veil we might notice a gap.
We can sense something is missing.

We still say nothing.

It is in the unwritten rules of propriety
To withhold our truth.

VICTORY

A lifetime of wanting

A lifetime of training

A lifetime of waiting

A moment of winning.

Forever in history...

(Triple Crown winner, American Pharaoh)

VOWS

A moment in time.
A sense of completion.
Hearts are joined.
It is instantaneous.

Found in this vast universe.
Your Spirits are now one.
United.
Magnetized.
Committed to each other.

Lifetime partners
on life's journey.
Safe in the protection of each other.

The story is now one story.
This love is now one love.
In this moment of time.

(For Robert's Wedding)

WARUM?

(WHY?)
Madness knows no boundaries.
Madness knows no borders.

It festers unseen and unheard in the world.
Invisible, until it strikes out.
Exploding its venom.

Like a volcano
which destroys everything and anything in its path.

It is the face of evil
which disturbs our peace and shakes our complacency.

Finally recognized.

Random and devastating in its wake.

It leaves a footprint of inconsolable grief.

(The title is from a sign posted in a small German town's memorial for the students who died when the pilot intentionally crashed his plane into the Swiss Alps)

WHEN DEATH COMES CALLING

When Death comes calling, how will you be?

When the Angel of Death's arms wrap around you and
lift you out...
Will you go willingly?
Gently?
In sweet surrender?

How long will you linger at the door?
Will the sweetness of life reward you?
Or will bitterness and despair grab you and hold you
back?

How long will unfinished words keep you here?
Or can you soar?

Death has always been a mystery:
It comes announced.
It comes unannounced.
Yet it comes.

It is life's great tornado--
When Death comes calling.

WHEN YOU LEFT

I didn't know I loved you till you left.

I didn't know I felt that way until it was too late.

The words fall silently through my tears.

How could I not have known?

All those years of unsaid words.

Now you are gone.

I can no longer share my heart with you.

I can no longer tell you that I loved you,

Nor that I love you still.

WIZARD OF OZ...

I am on journey.

I am all the characters at once:

I am Dorothy...
I am on a journey of discovery.

I am the Wizard...
I am under the illusion that I can control everything.

I am the Tin Man...
I am looking for my heart.

I am the Scarecrow...
I am trying to reconnect my brain, my body and my heart.

I am the Lion...
I am desperately trying to find my courage.

(On surgery)

WOUNDED WARRIOR

You are standing guard:
Vigilant
Haunted
Horrified
Frightened.

Allow your mind to rest
Nurture it
Support it
Comfort it
Honor it.

Let it recover
Let it breathe
Allow it to stretch.

Allow it to open again.
Set it free.

Forgive the abuser
Forgive the atrocities
Save yourself.

You are not limited by those memories in your mind.

POST SCRIPT

It took courage for me to write these words.
It took courage for me to share them.
It took courage to be seen and to be vulnerable.
It took courage to step beyond my own limitations, my
personal terrors and fears. It took courage to allow
myself to feel more fully.

I am continuing to explore. I feel empowered.
Yes, I am a work-in-progress still.
My soul is speaking.

I am humbled and honored that you have read my poems.

Perhaps one of my poems resonated with you.
Perhaps you were puzzled.
Perhaps it revealed something.
Perhaps, perhaps, perhaps.

Anything which gets committed to the written word,
which is expressed, which comes to the light, has its
own energy and its own life.

These words, therefore, are no longer mine, but yours.

I entrust my words to you.

With love,

Vera

THEMES

FEAR:

AFTERMATH
BLITZKRIEG
NOISE IN MY HEAD
PARTICIPATION
SHOCKWAVE
WOUNDED WARRIOR
WIZARD OF OZ

HOSPITALIZATION:

ANGELS ON THE LOOSE
BROKEN HEART
CRISIS
FEAR
METAMORPHOSIS
PAIN
POST SURGERY
RECUPERATION
ROLLER COASTER
SECOND CHANCE
SUPPORT

ILLUSIONS:

ANACHRONISM
BLIND SPOT
CHAOS
DEFENSES
THE GAME
MEDDLING
MOVIE
PAPER BAG
PUPPETRY
STARDUST
STEAM ROLLER
TOXIC DUMP
THE VEIL

IN LOVING MEMORY:

DID I TOUCH YOU?
DO YOU KNOW ME?
If I DIE BEFORE YOU
LOST SOULS
MELODIES
STANDING IN THE RAIN
WHEN YOU LEFT

LOSS:

CHILDLESS
THE DANCE
END OF THE ROAD
FORGIVENESS
THE JUKE BOX
LOVING YOU
MISSING YOU
REVELATION

SOUL:

THE FOREST OF MY SOUL
METAMORPHOSIS
THE VOICE OF THE SOUL

WITNESS:

AMERICAN DREAM
DESPERATION
ENDANGERED SPECIES
ICH BIN JUDE
SLAVES
STOLEN BODIES
TIME STANDS STILL
VICTORY
VOWS
WARUM
WOUNDED WARRIOR

OVATIONS

Read why these professionals find Vera's writing so moving...

"Vera's writings have passed through the guarded gates of her Soul. They present as words that may touch and bring Light to so many. Who is to say Who is a writer? When the portal opens we all well might be the poet laureate of our own heart".
—Harriett Simon Salinger MCC, LCSW
WiseWoman Coaching
Certificate in Spiritual Direction

"Vera's poetry touches my very core, provoking thoughts that gnaw and resonate. Her insights of life, death, aging, truth and more leave me on an emotional cliff. The more I read, the more deeply I feel. This is the first compendium of a great body of work. I believe, like me, you'll yearn for more."
—Susi P

"The world has been missing this collection. Within her poetry, Vera captures the raw feelings within us all. Then, in a magical dance of words and wisdom, Vera conveys these visceral perceptions with a cerebral resonance that set both the heart and mind at peace."
—Jill

"Vera's work is deeply heart felt, at times heart wrenching and always resonate with universal feelings."
—Dr Robert Abramson, MD

"Vera's words always reflect poignant insights into the challenges and joys of living. Reading her thoughts will, I am sure, serve as a catalyst stimulating deeper exploration of your own."
—Michele O'Neal, Retired Mental Health Administrator

"Vera Stasny's poems reach readers with both raw intimacy and empathetic calm.This combination of honesty with kindness creates a strength into which readers can gratefully lean. A pleasure to read."
—Marilyn Davis, writing instructor at California State University, at Fullerton, and author of Green Leaf Places: poems and lyrics.

"Reading Vera Stasny's poetry helped me connect even more deeply to my own journey. Through her vulnerability as a writer I've been able to tap into and validate feelings I hadn't yet expressed—even to myself. As I read each poem I found myself pausing to savor and reflect. Thank you for sharing your gift."
—Karen

Printed in the United States
By Bookmasters